Christmas CARD LIST

A Six-Year Address Book & Tracker for Holiday Card Mailings

PRISMATIC PUBLICATIONS
LOS ANGELES

Designed by Prismatic Publications
Graphic elements by Pixabay, Freepik, Deposit Photos

Copyright ©2017
Prismatic Publications
All rights reserved
ISBN 978-1-943986-30-9
Printed in in USA

www.JournalsOnAmazon.com

Happy Holidays

'Tis the season to put pen to paper and send out your annual Christmas cards. This address book & log makes keeping track of the cards you send and receive a snap. The book is organized alphabetically, with 36 entries for each letter (PQ & XYZ are combined) and six years of tracking. A section for notes can be found at the back. Here's a sample of holiday greetings to get your creative juices flowing. Mix and match or customize however you like!

Tidings

- May this Christmas season bring you closer to all those who you treasure in your heart. Have a Merry Christmas and a Happy New year!

- Love, joy and peace are the ingredients for a wonderful Christmas. We hope you find them all festive season. Have a Merry Christmas and a Happy New year!

- May you find more smiles on your face this Christmas than ever before. Wishing you and your family a Merry Christmas and a Happy New Year! Make it grand!

- May your Christmas sparkle with moments of love, laughter and goodwill, and may the year ahead be full of contentment and joy. Have a rocking Christmas.

- I'm glad to have people like you in my life to send Christmas cards. I am truly blessed this Christmas!

- It's the time of eggnog, candles, cakes, songs, reindeer, carols, laughter — and most importantly LOVE. Merry Christmas.

- Let the spirit of love gently fill our hearts and homes. In this loveliest of seasons may you find many reasons for happiness.

Short & Sweet

- Wishing your family all the jingly, jolly joys of Christmas.

- Merry Christmas with all the trimmings!

- Have a magical holiday season.

- Decorate your Christmas with joy!

- Wishing you all the joy, hope and wonder of Christmas!

- Blessings, love, and peace to you this Christmas.

- May peace, love and prosperity follow you always.

Quotes

❄ Christmas waves a magic wand over this world, and behold, everything softer and more beautiful. ~*Norman Vincent Peale*

❄ I will honor Christmas in my heart, and try to keep it all the year. ~*Charles Dickens*

❄ Our hearts grow tender with childhood memories and love of kindred, and we are better throughout the year for having, in spirit, become a child again at Christmas-time. ~*Laura Ingalls Wilder*

❄ 'Maybe Christmas', he thought, 'doesn't come from a store. Maybe Christmas, perhaps, means a little bit more!' ~*Dr. Seuss*

❄ At Christmas, all roads lead home. ~*Marjorie Holmes*

❄ It is Christmas in the heart that puts Christmas in the air. ~*W.T. Ellis*

Religious

❄ For unto us a child is born... ~Isaiah 9:6

❄ May God bless your home with peace, joy and love. Have a merry Christmas!

❄ Remember that the reason for the season is the reason all the time. Merry Christmas!

❄ May you feel the love of Christ this Christmas!

❄ Today in the town of David a Savior has been born to you; he is Christ the Lord. ~Luke 2:11

❄ May the Good Lord fulfill you with His promises and bestow on you His many blessings.

Closings

❄ Wishing you joy,

❄ Blessings,

❄ Joy for your day,

❄ Cheerfully in Christ,

❄ Peace be with you,

❄ Brightest blessings,

❄ Warmest wishes,

❄ Grace and peace,

Discover more journals for your life!

www.JournalsOnAmazon.com

NAME		YEAR							A
ADDRESS		SENT	○	○	○	○	○	○	
		RCVD	○	○	○	○	○	○	
NAME		YEAR							
ADDRESS		SENT	○	○	○	○	○	○	
		RCVD	○	○	○	○	○	○	
NAME		YEAR							
ADDRESS		SENT	○	○	○	○	○	○	
		RCVD	○	○	○	○	○	○	
NAME		YEAR							
ADDRESS		SENT	○	○	○	○	○	○	
		RCVD	○	○	○	○	○	○	
NAME		YEAR							
ADDRESS		SENT	○	○	○	○	○	○	
		RCVD	○	○	○	○	○	○	
NAME		YEAR							
ADDRESS		SENT	○	○	○	○	○	○	
		RCVD	○	○	○	○	○	○	
NAME		YEAR							
ADDRESS		SENT	○	○	○	○	○	○	
		RCVD	○	○	○	○	○	○	
NAME		YEAR							
ADDRESS		SENT	○	○	○	○	○	○	
		RCVD	○	○	○	○	○	○	
NAME		YEAR							
ADDRESS		SENT	○	○	○	○	○	○	
		RCVD	○	○	○	○	○	○	

NAME		YEAR						
ADDRESS	8509? Falcon Ridge Trail Brooksville FL 34602	SENT	○	○	○	○	○	○
		RCVD	○	○	○	○	○	○
NAME		YEAR						
ADDRESS		SENT	○	○	○	○	○	○
		RCVD	○	○	○	○	○	○
NAME		YEAR						
ADDRESS		SENT	○	○	○	○	○	○
		RCVD	○	○	○	○	○	○
NAME		YEAR						
ADDRESS		SENT	○	○	○	○	○	○
		RCVD	○	○	○	○	○	○
NAME		YEAR						
ADDRESS		SENT	○	○	○	○	○	○
		RCVD	○	○	○	○	○	○
NAME		YEAR						
ADDRESS		SENT	○	○	○	○	○	○
		RCVD	○	○	○	○	○	○
NAME		YEAR						
ADDRESS		SENT	○	○	○	○	○	○
		RCVD	○	○	○	○	○	○
NAME		YEAR						
ADDRESS		SENT	○	○	○	○	○	○
		RCVD	○	○	○	○	○	○
NAME		YEAR						
ADDRESS		SENT	○	○	○	○	○	○
		RCVD	○	○	○	○	○	○

A

NAME		YEAR						
ADDRESS		SENT	○	○	○	○	○	○
		RCVD	○	○	○	○	○	○
NAME		YEAR						
ADDRESS		SENT	○	○	○	○	○	○
		RCVD	○	○	○	○	○	○
NAME		YEAR						
ADDRESS		SENT	○	○	○	○	○	○
		RCVD	○	○	○	○	○	○
NAME		YEAR						
ADDRESS		SENT	○	○	○	○	○	○
		RCVD	○	○	○	○	○	○
NAME		YEAR						
ADDRESS		SENT	○	○	○	○	○	○
		RCVD	○	○	○	○	○	○
NAME		YEAR						
ADDRESS		SENT	○	○	○	○	○	○
		RCVD	○	○	○	○	○	○
NAME		YEAR						
ADDRESS		SENT	○	○	○	○	○	○
		RCVD	○	○	○	○	○	○
NAME		YEAR						
ADDRESS		SENT	○	○	○	○	○	○
		RCVD	○	○	○	○	○	○
NAME		YEAR						
ADDRESS		SENT	○	○	○	○	○	○
		RCVD	○	○	○	○	○	○

B

NAME		YEAR					
ADDRESS		SENT	○	○	○	○	○	○
		RCVD	○	○	○	○	○	○
NAME		YEAR					
ADDRESS		SENT	○	○	○	○	○	○
		RCVD	○	○	○	○	○	○
NAME		YEAR					
ADDRESS		SENT	○	○	○	○	○	○
		RCVD	○	○	○	○	○	○
NAME		YEAR					
ADDRESS		SENT	○	○	○	○	○	○
		RCVD	○	○	○	○	○	○
NAME		YEAR					
ADDRESS		SENT	○	○	○	○	○	○
		RCVD	○	○	○	○	○	○
NAME		YEAR					
ADDRESS		SENT	○	○	○	○	○	○
		RCVD	○	○	○	○	○	○
NAME		YEAR					
ADDRESS		SENT	○	○	○	○	○	○
		RCVD	○	○	○	○	○	○
NAME		YEAR					
ADDRESS		SENT	○	○	○	○	○	○
		RCVD	○	○	○	○	○	○
NAME		YEAR					
ADDRESS		SENT	○	○	○	○	○	○
		RCVD	○	○	○	○	○	○

B

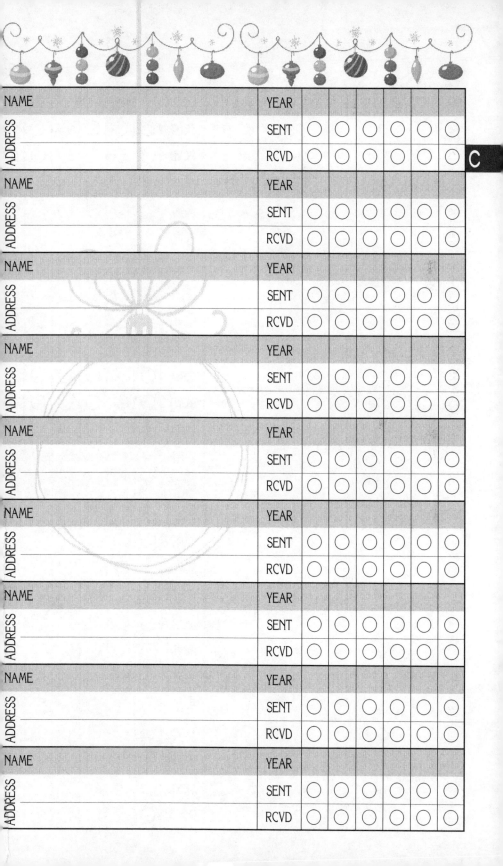

NAME		YEAR						
ADDRESS		SENT	○	○	○	○	○	○
		RCVD	○	○	○	○	○	○
NAME		YEAR						
ADDRESS		SENT	○	○	○	○	○	○
		RCVD	○	○	○	○	○	○
NAME		YEAR						
ADDRESS		SENT	○	○	○	○	○	○
		RCVD	○	○	○	○	○	○
NAME		YEAR						
ADDRESS		SENT	○	○	○	○	○	○
		RCVD	○	○	○	○	○	○
NAME		YEAR						
ADDRESS		SENT	○	○	○	○	○	○
		RCVD	○	○	○	○	○	○
NAME		YEAR						
ADDRESS		SENT	○	○	○	○	○	○
		RCVD	○	○	○	○	○	○
NAME		YEAR						
ADDRESS		SENT	○	○	○	○	○	○
		RCVD	○	○	○	○	○	○
NAME		YEAR						
ADDRESS		SENT	○	○	○	○	○	○
		RCVD	○	○	○	○	○	○
NAME		YEAR						
ADDRESS		SENT	○	○	○	○	○	○
		RCVD	○	○	○	○	○	○

C

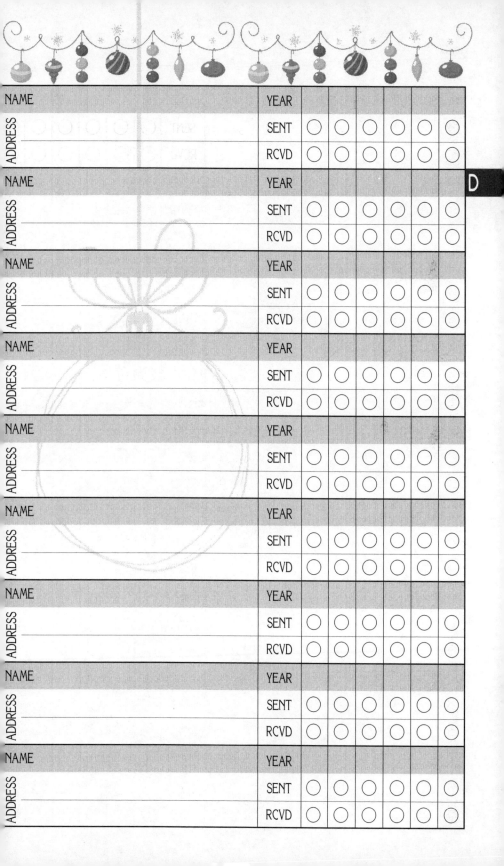

NAME		YEAR						
ADDRESS		SENT	○	○	○	○	○	○
		RCVD	○	○	○	○	○	○
NAME		YEAR						
ADDRESS		SENT	○	○	○	○	○	○
		RCVD	○	○	○	○	○	○
NAME		YEAR						
ADDRESS		SENT	○	○	○	○	○	○
		RCVD	○	○	○	○	○	○
NAME		YEAR						
ADDRESS		SENT	○	○	○	○	○	○
		RCVD	○	○	○	○	○	○
NAME		YEAR						
ADDRESS		SENT	○	○	○	○	○	○
		RCVD	○	○	○	○	○	○
NAME		YEAR						
ADDRESS		SENT	○	○	○	○	○	○
		RCVD	○	○	○	○	○	○
NAME		YEAR						
ADDRESS		SENT	○	○	○	○	○	○
		RCVD	○	○	○	○	○	○
NAME		YEAR						
ADDRESS		SENT	○	○	○	○	○	○
		RCVD	○	○	○	○	○	○
NAME		YEAR						
ADDRESS		SENT	○	○	○	○	○	○
		RCVD	○	○	○	○	○	○

D

NAME		YEAR						
ADDRESS		SENT	○	○	○	○	○	○
		RCVD	○	○	○	○	○	○
NAME		YEAR						
ADDRESS		SENT	○	○	○	○	○	○
		RCVD	○	○	○	○	○	○
NAME		YEAR						
ADDRESS		SENT	○	○	○	○	○	○
		RCVD	○	○	○	○	○	○
NAME		YEAR						
ADDRESS		SENT	○	○	○	○	○	○
		RCVD	○	○	○	○	○	○
NAME		YEAR						
ADDRESS		SENT	○	○	○	○	○	○
		RCVD	○	○	○	○	○	○
NAME		YEAR						
ADDRESS		SENT	○	○	○	○	○	○
		RCVD	○	○	○	○	○	○
NAME		YEAR						
ADDRESS		SENT	○	○	○	○	○	○
		RCVD	○	○	○	○	○	○
NAME		YEAR						
ADDRESS		SENT	○	○	○	○	○	○
		RCVD	○	○	○	○	○	○
NAME		YEAR						
ADDRESS		SENT	○	○	○	○	○	○
		RCVD	○	○	○	○	○	○

E

NAME		YEAR						
ADDRESS		SENT	○	○	○	○	○	○
		RCVD	○	○	○	○	○	○
NAME		YEAR						
ADDRESS		SENT	○	○	○	○	○	○
		RCVD	○	○	○	○	○	○
NAME		YEAR						
ADDRESS		SENT	○	○	○	○	○	○
		RCVD	○	○	○	○	○	○
NAME		YEAR						
ADDRESS		SENT	○	○	○	○	○	○
		RCVD	○	○	○	○	○	○
NAME		YEAR						
ADDRESS		SENT	○	○	○	○	○	○
		RCVD	○	○	○	○	○	○
NAME		YEAR						
ADDRESS		SENT	○	○	○	○	○	○
		RCVD	○	○	○	○	○	○
NAME		YEAR						
ADDRESS		SENT	○	○	○	○	○	○
		RCVD	○	○	○	○	○	○
NAME		YEAR						
ADDRESS		SENT	○	○	○	○	○	○
		RCVD	○	○	○	○	○	○
NAME		YEAR						
ADDRESS		SENT	○	○	○	○	○	○
		RCVD	○	○	○	○	○	○

NAME		YEAR						
ADDRESS		SENT	○	○	○	○	○	○
		RCVD	○	○	○	○	○	○
NAME		YEAR						
ADDRESS		SENT	○	○	○	○	○	○
		RCVD	○	○	○	○	○	○
NAME		YEAR						
ADDRESS		SENT	○	○	○	○	○	○
		RCVD	○	○	○	○	○	○
NAME		YEAR						
ADDRESS		SENT	○	○	○	○	○	○
		RCVD	○	○	○	○	○	○
NAME		YEAR						
ADDRESS		SENT	○	○	○	○	○	○
		RCVD	○	○	○	○	○	○
NAME		YEAR						
ADDRESS		SENT	○	○	○	○	○	○
		RCVD	○	○	○	○	○	○
NAME		YEAR						
ADDRESS		SENT	○	○	○	○	○	○
		RCVD	○	○	○	○	○	○
NAME		YEAR						
ADDRESS		SENT	○	○	○	○	○	○
		RCVD	○	○	○	○	○	○
NAME		YEAR						
ADDRESS		SENT	○	○	○	○	○	○
		RCVD	○	○	○	○	○	○

F

NAME		YEAR						
ADDRESS		SENT	○	○	○	○	○	○
		RCVD	○	○	○	○	○	○
NAME		YEAR						
ADDRESS		SENT	○	○	○	○	○	○
		RCVD	○	○	○	○	○	○
NAME		YEAR						
ADDRESS		SENT	○	○	○	○	○	○
		RCVD	○	○	○	○	○	○
NAME		YEAR						
ADDRESS		SENT	○	○	○	○	○	○
		RCVD	○	○	○	○	○	○
NAME		YEAR						
ADDRESS		SENT	○	○	○	○	○	○
		RCVD	○	○	○	○	○	○
NAME		YEAR						
ADDRESS		SENT	○	○	○	○	○	○
		RCVD	○	○	○	○	○	○
NAME		YEAR						
ADDRESS		SENT	○	○	○	○	○	○
		RCVD	○	○	○	○	○	○
NAME		YEAR						
ADDRESS		SENT	○	○	○	○	○	○
		RCVD	○	○	○	○	○	○
NAME		YEAR						
ADDRESS		SENT	○	○	○	○	○	○
		RCVD	○	○	○	○	○	○

NAME		YEAR						
ADDRESS		SENT	○	○	○	○	○	○
		RCVD	○	○	○	○	○	○
NAME		YEAR						
ADDRESS		SENT	○	○	○	○	○	○
		RCVD	○	○	○	○	○	○
NAME		YEAR						
ADDRESS		SENT	○	○	○	○	○	○
		RCVD	○	○	○	○	○	○
NAME		YEAR						
ADDRESS		SENT	○	○	○	○	○	○
		RCVD	○	○	○	○	○	○
NAME		YEAR						
ADDRESS		SENT	○	○	○	○	○	○
		RCVD	○	○	○	○	○	○
NAME		YEAR						
ADDRESS		SENT	○	○	○	○	○	○
		RCVD	○	○	○	○	○	○
NAME		YEAR						
ADDRESS		SENT	○	○	○	○	○	○
		RCVD	○	○	○	○	○	○
NAME		YEAR						
ADDRESS		SENT	○	○	○	○	○	○
		RCVD	○	○	○	○	○	○
NAME		YEAR						
ADDRESS		SENT	○	○	○	○	○	○
		RCVD	○	○	○	○	○	○

G

NAME		YEAR					
ADDRESS		SENT	○	○	○	○	○	○
		RCVD	○	○	○	○	○	○
NAME		YEAR					
ADDRESS		SENT	○	○	○	○	○	○
		RCVD	○	○	○	○	○	○
NAME		YEAR					
ADDRESS		SENT	○	○	○	○	○	○
		RCVD	○	○	○	○	○	○
NAME		YEAR					
ADDRESS		SENT	○	○	○	○	○	○
		RCVD	○	○	○	○	○	○
NAME		YEAR					
ADDRESS		SENT	○	○	○	○	○	○
		RCVD	○	○	○	○	○	○
NAME		YEAR					
ADDRESS		SENT	○	○	○	○	○	○
		RCVD	○	○	○	○	○	○
NAME		YEAR					
ADDRESS		SENT	○	○	○	○	○	○
		RCVD	○	○	○	○	○	○
NAME		YEAR					
ADDRESS		SENT	○	○	○	○	○	○
		RCVD	○	○	○	○	○	○
NAME		YEAR					
ADDRESS		SENT	○	○	○	○	○	○
		RCVD	○	○	○	○	○	○

NAME		YEAR						
ADDRESS		SENT	○	○	○	○	○	○
		RCVD	○	○	○	○	○	○
NAME		YEAR						
ADDRESS		SENT	○	○	○	○	○	○
		RCVD	○	○	○	○	○	○
NAME		YEAR						
ADDRESS		SENT	○	○	○	○	○	○
		RCVD	○	○	○	○	○	○
NAME		YEAR						
ADDRESS		SENT	○	○	○	○	○	○
		RCVD	○	○	○	○	○	○
NAME		YEAR						
ADDRESS		SENT	○	○	○	○	○	○
		RCVD	○	○	○	○	○	○
NAME		YEAR						
ADDRESS		SENT	○	○	○	○	○	○
		RCVD	○	○	○	○	○	○
NAME		YEAR						
ADDRESS		SENT	○	○	○	○	○	○
		RCVD	○	○	○	○	○	○
NAME		YEAR						
ADDRESS		SENT	○	○	○	○	○	○
		RCVD	○	○	○	○	○	○
NAME		YEAR						
ADDRESS		SENT	○	○	○	○	○	○
		RCVD	○	○	○	○	○	○

H

NAME		YEAR						
ADDRESS		SENT	○	○	○	○	○	○
		RCVD	○	○	○	○	○	○
NAME		YEAR						
ADDRESS		SENT	○	○	○	○	○	○
		RCVD	○	○	○	○	○	○
NAME		YEAR						
ADDRESS		SENT	○	○	○	○	○	○
		RCVD	○	○	○	○	○	○
NAME		YEAR						
ADDRESS		SENT	○	○	○	○	○	○
		RCVD	○	○	○	○	○	○
NAME		YEAR						
ADDRESS		SENT	○	○	○	○	○	○
		RCVD	○	○	○	○	○	○
NAME		YEAR						
ADDRESS		SENT	○	○	○	○	○	○
		RCVD	○	○	○	○	○	○
NAME		YEAR						
ADDRESS		SENT	○	○	○	○	○	○
		RCVD	○	○	○	○	○	○
NAME		YEAR						
ADDRESS		SENT	○	○	○	○	○	○
		RCVD	○	○	○	○	○	○
NAME		YEAR						
ADDRESS		SENT	○	○	○	○	○	○
		RCVD	○	○	○	○	○	○

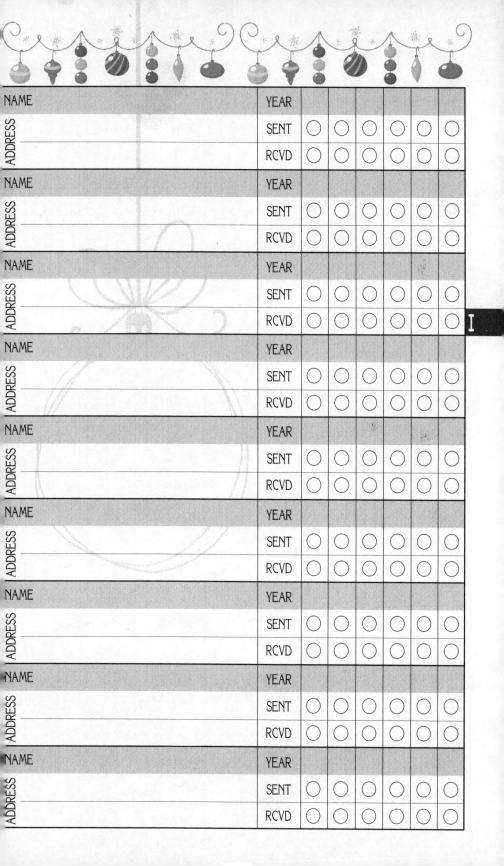

NAME		YEAR						
ADDRESS		SENT	○	○	○	○	○	○
		RCVD	○	○	○	○	○	○
NAME		YEAR						
ADDRESS		SENT	○	○	○	○	○	○
		RCVD	○	○	○	○	○	○
NAME		YEAR						
ADDRESS		SENT	○	○	○	○	○	○
		RCVD	○	○	○	○	○	○
NAME		YEAR						
ADDRESS		SENT	○	○	○	○	○	○
		RCVD	○	○	○	○	○	○
NAME		YEAR						
ADDRESS		SENT	○	○	○	○	○	○
		RCVD	○	○	○	○	○	○
NAME		YEAR						
ADDRESS		SENT	○	○	○	○	○	○
		RCVD	○	○	○	○	○	○
NAME		YEAR						
ADDRESS		SENT	○	○	○	○	○	○
		RCVD	○	○	○	○	○	○
NAME		YEAR						
ADDRESS		SENT	○	○	○	○	○	○
		RCVD	○	○	○	○	○	○
NAME		YEAR						
ADDRESS		SENT	○	○	○	○	○	○
		RCVD	○	○	○	○	○	○

NAME		YEAR						
ADDRESS		SENT	○	○	○	○	○	○
		RCVD	○	○	○	○	○	○
NAME		YEAR						
ADDRESS		SENT	○	○	○	○	○	○
		RCVD	○	○	○	○	○	○
NAME		YEAR						
ADDRESS		SENT	○	○	○	○	○	○
		RCVD	○	○	○	○	○	○
NAME		YEAR						
ADDRESS		SENT	○	○	○	○	○	○
		RCVD	○	○	○	○	○	○
NAME		YEAR						
ADDRESS		SENT	○	○	○	○	○	○
		RCVD	○	○	○	○	○	○
NAME		YEAR						
ADDRESS		SENT	○	○	○	○	○	○
		RCVD	○	○	○	○	○	○
NAME		YEAR						
ADDRESS		SENT	○	○	○	○	○	○
		RCVD	○	○	○	○	○	○
NAME		YEAR						
ADDRESS		SENT	○	○	○	○	○	○
		RCVD	○	○	○	○	○	○
NAME		YEAR						
ADDRESS		SENT	○	○	○	○	○	○
		RCVD	○	○	○	○	○	○

NAME		YEAR						
ADDRESS		SENT	○	○	○	○	○	○
		RCVD	○	○	○	○	○	○
NAME		YEAR						
ADDRESS		SENT	○	○	○	○	○	○
		RCVD	○	○	○	○	○	○
NAME		YEAR						
ADDRESS		SENT	○	○	○	○	○	○
		RCVD	○	○	○	○	○	○
NAME		YEAR						
ADDRESS		SENT	○	○	○	○	○	○
		RCVD	○	○	○	○	○	○
NAME		YEAR						
ADDRESS		SENT	○	○	○	○	○	○
		RCVD	○	○	○	○	○	○
NAME		YEAR						
ADDRESS		SENT	○	○	○	○	○	○
		RCVD	○	○	○	○	○	○
NAME		YEAR						
ADDRESS		SENT	○	○	○	○	○	○
		RCVD	○	○	○	○	○	○
NAME		YEAR						
ADDRESS		SENT	○	○	○	○	○	○
		RCVD	○	○	○	○	○	○
NAME		YEAR						
ADDRESS		SENT	○	○	○	○	○	○
		RCVD	○	○	○	○	○	○

I

NAME		YEAR						
ADDRESS		SENT	○	○	○	○	○	○
		RCVD	○	○	○	○	○	○
NAME		YEAR						
ADDRESS		SENT	○	○	○	○	○	○
		RCVD	○	○	○	○	○	○
NAME		YEAR						
ADDRESS		SENT	○	○	○	○	○	○
		RCVD	○	○	○	○	○	○
NAME		YEAR						
ADDRESS		SENT	○	○	○	○	○	○
		RCVD	○	○	○	○	○	○
NAME		YEAR						
ADDRESS		SENT	○	○	○	○	○	○
		RCVD	○	○	○	○	○	○
NAME		YEAR						
ADDRESS		SENT	○	○	○	○	○	○
		RCVD	○	○	○	○	○	○
NAME		YEAR						
ADDRESS		SENT	○	○	○	○	○	○
		RCVD	○	○	○	○	○	○
NAME		YEAR						
ADDRESS		SENT	○	○	○	○	○	○
		RCVD	○	○	○	○	○	○
NAME		YEAR						
ADDRESS		SENT	○	○	○	○	○	○
		RCVD	○	○	○	○	○	○

J

NAME		YEAR					
ADDRESS		SENT	○	○	○	○	○	○
		RCVD	○	○	○	○	○	○
NAME		YEAR					
ADDRESS		SENT	○	○	○	○	○	○
		RCVD	○	○	○	○	○	○
NAME		YEAR					
ADDRESS		SENT	○	○	○	○	○	○
		RCVD	○	○	○	○	○	○
NAME		YEAR					
ADDRESS		SENT	○	○	○	○	○	○
		RCVD	○	○	○	○	○	○
NAME		YEAR					
ADDRESS		SENT	○	○	○	○	○	○
		RCVD	○	○	○	○	○	○
NAME		YEAR					
ADDRESS		SENT	○	○	○	○	○	○
		RCVD	○	○	○	○	○	○
NAME		YEAR					
ADDRESS		SENT	○	○	○	○	○	○
		RCVD	○	○	○	○	○	○
NAME		YEAR					
ADDRESS		SENT	○	○	○	○	○	○
		RCVD	○	○	○	○	○	○
NAME		YEAR					
ADDRESS		SENT	○	○	○	○	○	○
		RCVD	○	○	○	○	○	○

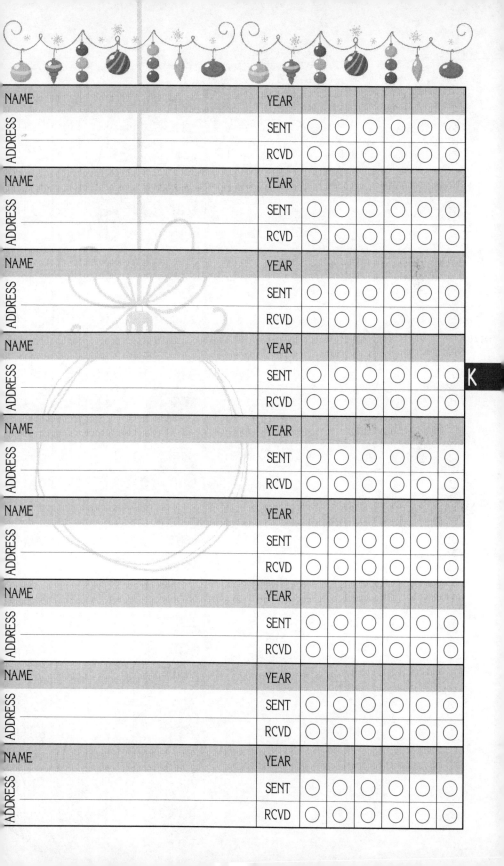

NAME		YEAR						
ADDRESS		SENT	○	○	○	○	○	○
		RCVD	○	○	○	○	○	○
NAME		YEAR						
ADDRESS		SENT	○	○	○	○	○	○
		RCVD	○	○	○	○	○	○
NAME		YEAR						
ADDRESS		SENT	○	○	○	○	○	○
		RCVD	○	○	○	○	○	○
NAME		YEAR						
ADDRESS		SENT	○	○	○	○	○	○
		RCVD	○	○	○	○	○	○
NAME		YEAR						
ADDRESS		SENT	○	○	○	○	○	○
		RCVD	○	○	○	○	○	○
NAME		YEAR						
ADDRESS		SENT	○	○	○	○	○	○
		RCVD	○	○	○	○	○	○
NAME		YEAR						
ADDRESS		SENT	○	○	○	○	○	○
		RCVD	○	○	○	○	○	○
NAME		YEAR						
ADDRESS		SENT	○	○	○	○	○	○
		RCVD	○	○	○	○	○	○
NAME		YEAR						
ADDRESS		SENT	○	○	○	○	○	○
		RCVD	○	○	○	○	○	○

K

NAME		YEAR						
ADDRESS		SENT	○	○	○	○	○	○
		RCVD	○	○	○	○	○	○
NAME		YEAR						
ADDRESS		SENT	○	○	○	○	○	○
		RCVD	○	○	○	○	○	○
NAME		YEAR						
ADDRESS		SENT	○	○	○	○	○	○
		RCVD	○	○	○	○	○	○
NAME		YEAR						
ADDRESS		SENT	○	○	○	○	○	○
		RCVD	○	○	○	○	○	○
NAME		YEAR						
ADDRESS		SENT	○	○	○	○	○	○
		RCVD	○	○	○	○	○	○
NAME		YEAR						
ADDRESS		SENT	○	○	○	○	○	○
		RCVD	○	○	○	○	○	○
NAME		YEAR						
ADDRESS		SENT	○	○	○	○	○	○
		RCVD	○	○	○	○	○	○
NAME		YEAR						
ADDRESS		SENT	○	○	○	○	○	○
		RCVD	○	○	○	○	○	○
NAME		YEAR						
ADDRESS		SENT	○	○	○	○	○	○
		RCVD	○	○	○	○	○	○

NAME		YEAR						
ADDRESS		SENT	○	○	○	○	○	○
		RCVD	○	○	○	○	○	○
NAME		YEAR						
ADDRESS		SENT	○	○	○	○	○	○
		RCVD	○	○	○	○	○	○
NAME		YEAR						
ADDRESS		SENT	○	○	○	○	○	○
		RCVD	○	○	○	○	○	○
NAME		YEAR						
ADDRESS		SENT	○	○	○	○	○	○
		RCVD	○	○	○	○	○	○
NAME		YEAR						
ADDRESS		SENT	○	○	○	○	○	○
		RCVD	○	○	○	○	○	○
NAME		YEAR						
ADDRESS		SENT	○	○	○	○	○	○
		RCVD	○	○	○	○	○	○
NAME		YEAR						
ADDRESS		SENT	○	○	○	○	○	○
		RCVD	○	○	○	○	○	○
NAME		YEAR						
ADDRESS		SENT	○	○	○	○	○	○
		RCVD	○	○	○	○	○	○
NAME		YEAR						
ADDRESS		SENT	○	○	○	○	○	○
		RCVD	○	○	○	○	○	○

L

NAME		YEAR						
ADDRESS		SENT	○	○	○	○	○	○
		RCVD	○	○	○	○	○	○
NAME		YEAR						
ADDRESS		SENT	○	○	○	○	○	○
		RCVD	○	○	○	○	○	○
NAME		YEAR						
ADDRESS		SENT	○	○	○	○	○	○
		RCVD	○	○	○	○	○	○
NAME		YEAR						
ADDRESS		SENT	○	○	○	○	○	○
		RCVD	○	○	○	○	○	○
NAME		YEAR						
ADDRESS		SENT	○	○	○	○	○	○
		RCVD	○	○	○	○	○	○
NAME		YEAR						
ADDRESS		SENT	○	○	○	○	○	○
		RCVD	○	○	○	○	○	○
NAME		YEAR						
ADDRESS		SENT	○	○	○	○	○	○
		RCVD	○	○	○	○	○	○
NAME		YEAR						
ADDRESS		SENT	○	○	○	○	○	○
		RCVD	○	○	○	○	○	○
NAME		YEAR						
ADDRESS		SENT	○	○	○	○	○	○
		RCVD	○	○	○	○	○	○

M

NAME		YEAR						
ADDRESS		SENT	○	○	○	○	○	○
		RCVD	○	○	○	○	○	○
NAME		YEAR						
ADDRESS		SENT	○	○	○	○	○	○
		RCVD	○	○	○	○	○	○
NAME		YEAR						
ADDRESS		SENT	○	○	○	○	○	○
		RCVD	○	○	○	○	○	○
NAME		YEAR						
ADDRESS		SENT	○	○	○	○	○	○
		RCVD	○	○	○	○	○	○
NAME		YEAR						
ADDRESS		SENT	○	○	○	○	○	○
		RCVD	○	○	○	○	○	○
NAME		YEAR						
ADDRESS		SENT	○	○	○	○	○	○
		RCVD	○	○	○	○	○	○
NAME		YEAR						
ADDRESS		SENT	○	○	○	○	○	○
		RCVD	○	○	○	○	○	○
NAME		YEAR						
ADDRESS		SENT	○	○	○	○	○	○
		RCVD	○	○	○	○	○	○
NAME		YEAR						
ADDRESS		SENT	○	○	○	○	○	○
		RCVD	○	○	○	○	○	○

M

NAME		YEAR						
ADDRESS		SENT	○	○	○	○	○	○
		RCVD	○	○	○	○	○	○
NAME		YEAR						
ADDRESS		SENT	○	○	○	○	○	○
		RCVD	○	○	○	○	○	○
NAME		YEAR						
ADDRESS		SENT	○	○	○	○	○	○
		RCVD	○	○	○	○	○	○
NAME		YEAR						
ADDRESS		SENT	○	○	○	○	○	○
		RCVD	○	○	○	○	○	○
NAME		YEAR						
ADDRESS		SENT	○	○	○	○	○	○
		RCVD	○	○	○	○	○	○
NAME		YEAR						
ADDRESS		SENT	○	○	○	○	○	○
		RCVD	○	○	○	○	○	○
NAME		YEAR						
ADDRESS		SENT	○	○	○	○	○	○
		RCVD	○	○	○	○	○	○
NAME		YEAR						
ADDRESS		SENT	○	○	○	○	○	○
		RCVD	○	○	○	○	○	○
NAME		YEAR						
ADDRESS		SENT	○	○	○	○	○	○
		RCVD	○	○	○	○	○	○

N

NAME		YEAR						
ADDRESS		SENT	○	○	○	○	○	○
		RCVD	○	○	○	○	○	○
NAME		YEAR						
ADDRESS		SENT	○	○	○	○	○	○
		RCVD	○	○	○	○	○	○
NAME		YEAR						
ADDRESS		SENT	○	○	○	○	○	○
		RCVD	○	○	○	○	○	○
NAME		YEAR						
ADDRESS		SENT	○	○	○	○	○	○
		RCVD	○	○	○	○	○	○
NAME		YEAR						
ADDRESS		SENT	○	○	○	○	○	○
		RCVD	○	○	○	○	○	○
NAME		YEAR						
ADDRESS		SENT	○	○	○	○	○	○
		RCVD	○	○	○	○	○	○
NAME		YEAR						
ADDRESS		SENT	○	○	○	○	○	○
		RCVD	○	○	○	○	○	○
NAME		YEAR						
ADDRESS		SENT	○	○	○	○	○	○
		RCVD	○	○	○	○	○	○
NAME		YEAR						
ADDRESS		SENT	○	○	○	○	○	○
		RCVD	○	○	○	○	○	○

N

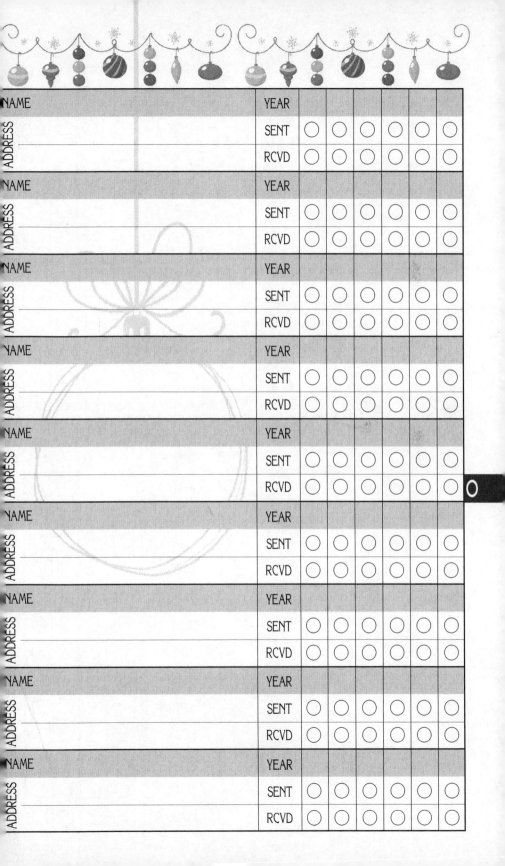

NAME		YEAR					
ADDRESS		SENT	○	○	○	○	○	○
		RCVD	○	○	○	○	○	○
NAME		YEAR					
ADDRESS		SENT	○	○	○	○	○	○
		RCVD	○	○	○	○	○	○
NAME		YEAR					
ADDRESS		SENT	○	○	○	○	○	○
		RCVD	○	○	○	○	○	○
NAME		YEAR					
ADDRESS		SENT	○	○	○	○	○	○
		RCVD	○	○	○	○	○	○
NAME		YEAR					
ADDRESS		SENT	○	○	○	○	○	○
		RCVD	○	○	○	○	○	○
NAME		YEAR					
ADDRESS		SENT	○	○	○	○	○	○
		RCVD	○	○	○	○	○	○
NAME		YEAR					
ADDRESS		SENT	○	○	○	○	○	○
		RCVD	○	○	○	○	○	○
NAME		YEAR					
ADDRESS		SENT	○	○	○	○	○	○
		RCVD	○	○	○	○	○	○
NAME		YEAR					
ADDRESS		SENT	○	○	○	○	○	○
		RCVD	○	○	○	○	○	○

NAME		YEAR						
ADDRESS		SENT	○	○	○	○	○	○
		RCVD	○	○	○	○	○	○
NAME		YEAR						
ADDRESS		SENT	○	○	○	○	○	○
		RCVD	○	○	○	○	○	○
NAME		YEAR						
ADDRESS		SENT	○	○	○	○	○	○
		RCVD	○	○	○	○	○	○
NAME		YEAR						
ADDRESS		SENT	○	○	○	○	○	○
		RCVD	○	○	○	○	○	○
NAME		YEAR						
ADDRESS		SENT	○	○	○	○	○	○
		RCVD	○	○	○	○	○	○
NAME		YEAR						
ADDRESS		SENT	○	○	○	○	○	○
		RCVD	○	○	○	○	○	○
NAME		YEAR						
ADDRESS		SENT	○	○	○	○	○	○
		RCVD	○	○	○	○	○	○
NAME		YEAR						
ADDRESS		SENT	○	○	○	○	○	○
		RCVD	○	○	○	○	○	○
NAME		YEAR						
ADDRESS		SENT	○	○	○	○	○	○
		RCVD	○	○	○	○	○	○

P
Q

NAME		YEAR						
ADDRESS		SENT	○	○	○	○	○	○
		RCVD	○	○	○	○	○	○
NAME		YEAR						
ADDRESS		SENT	○	○	○	○	○	○
		RCVD	○	○	○	○	○	○
NAME		YEAR						
ADDRESS		SENT	○	○	○	○	○	○
		RCVD	○	○	○	○	○	○
NAME		YEAR						
ADDRESS		SENT	○	○	○	○	○	○
		RCVD	○	○	○	○	○	○
NAME		YEAR						
ADDRESS		SENT	○	○	○	○	○	○
		RCVD	○	○	○	○	○	○
NAME		YEAR						
ADDRESS		SENT	○	○	○	○	○	○
		RCVD	○	○	○	○	○	○
NAME		YEAR						
ADDRESS		SENT	○	○	○	○	○	○
		RCVD	○	○	○	○	○	○
NAME		YEAR						
ADDRESS		SENT	○	○	○	○	○	○
		RCVD	○	○	○	○	○	○
NAME		YEAR						
ADDRESS		SENT	○	○	○	○	○	○
		RCVD	○	○	○	○	○	○

P Q

NAME		YEAR					
ADDRESS		SENT	○	○	○	○	○	○
		RCVD	○	○	○	○	○	○
NAME		YEAR					
ADDRESS		SENT	○	○	○	○	○	○
		RCVD	○	○	○	○	○	○
NAME		YEAR					
ADDRESS		SENT	○	○	○	○	○	○
		RCVD	○	○	○	○	○	○
NAME		YEAR					
ADDRESS		SENT	○	○	○	○	○	○
		RCVD	○	○	○	○	○	○
NAME		YEAR					
ADDRESS		SENT	○	○	○	○	○	○
		RCVD	○	○	○	○	○	○
NAME		YEAR					
ADDRESS		SENT	○	○	○	○	○	○
		RCVD	○	○	○	○	○	○
NAME		YEAR					
ADDRESS		SENT	○	○	○	○	○	○
		RCVD	○	○	○	○	○	○
NAME		YEAR					
ADDRESS		SENT	○	○	○	○	○	○
		RCVD	○	○	○	○	○	○
NAME		YEAR					
ADDRESS		SENT	○	○	○	○	○	○
		RCVD	○	○	○	○	○	○

R

NAME		YEAR						
ADDRESS		SENT	○	○	○	○	○	○
		RCVD	○	○	○	○	○	○
NAME		YEAR						
ADDRESS		SENT	○	○	○	○	○	○
		RCVD	○	○	○	○	○	○
NAME		YEAR						
ADDRESS		SENT	○	○	○	○	○	○
		RCVD	○	○	○	○	○	○
NAME		YEAR						
ADDRESS		SENT	○	○	○	○	○	○
		RCVD	○	○	○	○	○	○
NAME		YEAR						
ADDRESS		SENT	○	○	○	○	○	○
		RCVD	○	○	○	○	○	○
NAME		YEAR						
ADDRESS		SENT	○	○	○	○	○	○
		RCVD	○	○	○	○	○	○
NAME		YEAR						
ADDRESS		SENT	○	○	○	○	○	○
		RCVD	○	○	○	○	○	○
NAME		YEAR						
ADDRESS		SENT	○	○	○	○	○	○
		RCVD	○	○	○	○	○	○
NAME		YEAR						
ADDRESS		SENT	○	○	○	○	○	○
		RCVD	○	○	○	○	○	○

R

NAME		YEAR						
ADDRESS		SENT	○	○	○	○	○	○
		RCVD	○	○	○	○	○	○
NAME		YEAR						
ADDRESS		SENT	○	○	○	○	○	○
		RCVD	○	○	○	○	○	○
NAME		YEAR						
ADDRESS		SENT	○	○	○	○	○	○
		RCVD	○	○	○	○	○	○
NAME		YEAR						
ADDRESS		SENT	○	○	○	○	○	○
		RCVD	○	○	○	○	○	○
NAME		YEAR						
ADDRESS		SENT	○	○	○	○	○	○
		RCVD	○	○	○	○	○	○
NAME		YEAR						
ADDRESS		SENT	○	○	○	○	○	○
		RCVD	○	○	○	○	○	○
NAME		YEAR						
ADDRESS		SENT	○	○	○	○	○	○
		RCVD	○	○	○	○	○	○
NAME		YEAR						
ADDRESS		SENT	○	○	○	○	○	○
		RCVD	○	○	○	○	○	○
NAME		YEAR						
ADDRESS		SENT	○	○	○	○	○	○
		RCVD	○	○	○	○	○	○

S

NAME		YEAR						
ADDRESS		SENT	○	○	○	○	○	○
		RCVD	○	○	○	○	○	○
NAME		YEAR						
ADDRESS		SENT	○	○	○	○	○	○
		RCVD	○	○	○	○	○	○
NAME		YEAR						
ADDRESS		SENT	○	○	○	○	○	○
		RCVD	○	○	○	○	○	○
NAME		YEAR						
ADDRESS		SENT	○	○	○	○	○	○
		RCVD	○	○	○	○	○	○
NAME		YEAR						
ADDRESS		SENT	○	○	○	○	○	○
		RCVD	○	○	○	○	○	○
NAME		YEAR						
ADDRESS		SENT	○	○	○	○	○	○
		RCVD	○	○	○	○	○	○
NAME		YEAR						
ADDRESS		SENT	○	○	○	○	○	○
		RCVD	○	○	○	○	○	○
NAME		YEAR						
ADDRESS		SENT	○	○	○	○	○	○
		RCVD	○	○	○	○	○	○
NAME		YEAR						
ADDRESS		SENT	○	○	○	○	○	○
		RCVD	○	○	○	○	○	○

NAME		YEAR						
ADDRESS		SENT	○	○	○	○	○	○
		RCVD	○	○	○	○	○	○
NAME		YEAR						
ADDRESS		SENT	○	○	○	○	○	○
		RCVD	○	○	○	○	○	○
NAME		YEAR						
ADDRESS		SENT	○	○	○	○	○	○
		RCVD	○	○	○	○	○	○
NAME		YEAR						
ADDRESS		SENT	○	○	○	○	○	○
		RCVD	○	○	○	○	○	○
NAME		YEAR						
ADDRESS		SENT	○	○	○	○	○	○
		RCVD	○	○	○	○	○	○
NAME		YEAR						
ADDRESS		SENT	○	○	○	○	○	○
		RCVD	○	○	○	○	○	○
NAME		YEAR						
ADDRESS		SENT	○	○	○	○	○	○
		RCVD	○	○	○	○	○	○
NAME		YEAR						
ADDRESS		SENT	○	○	○	○	○	○
		RCVD	○	○	○	○	○	○
NAME		YEAR						
ADDRESS		SENT	○	○	○	○	○	○
		RCVD	○	○	○	○	○	○

T

NAME		YEAR						
ADDRESS		SENT	○	○	○	○	○	○
		RCVD	○	○	○	○	○	○
NAME		YEAR						
ADDRESS		SENT	○	○	○	○	○	○
		RCVD	○	○	○	○	○	○
NAME		YEAR						
ADDRESS		SENT	○	○	○	○	○	○
		RCVD	○	○	○	○	○	○
NAME		YEAR						
ADDRESS		SENT	○	○	○	○	○	○
		RCVD	○	○	○	○	○	○
NAME		YEAR						
ADDRESS		SENT	○	○	○	○	○	○
		RCVD	○	○	○	○	○	○
NAME		YEAR						
ADDRESS		SENT	○	○	○	○	○	○
		RCVD	○	○	○	○	○	○
NAME		YEAR						
ADDRESS		SENT	○	○	○	○	○	○
		RCVD	○	○	○	○	○	○
NAME		YEAR						
ADDRESS		SENT	○	○	○	○	○	○
		RCVD	○	○	○	○	○	○
NAME		YEAR						
ADDRESS		SENT	○	○	○	○	○	○
		RCVD	○	○	○	○	○	○

NAME			YEAR						
ADDRESS			SENT	○	○	○	○	○	○
			RCVD	○	○	○	○	○	○
NAME			YEAR						
ADDRESS			SENT	○	○	○	○	○	○
			RCVD	○	○	○	○	○	○
NAME			YEAR						
ADDRESS			SENT	○	○	○	○	○	○
			RCVD	○	○	○	○	○	○
NAME			YEAR						
ADDRESS			SENT	○	○	○	○	○	○
			RCVD	○	○	○	○	○	○
NAME			YEAR						
ADDRESS			SENT	○	○	○	○	○	○
			RCVD	○	○	○	○	○	○
NAME			YEAR						
ADDRESS			SENT	○	○	○	○	○	○
			RCVD	○	○	○	○	○	○
NAME			YEAR						
ADDRESS			SENT	○	○	○	○	○	○
			RCVD	○	○	○	○	○	○
NAME			YEAR						
ADDRESS			SENT	○	○	○	○	○	○
			RCVD	○	○	○	○	○	○
NAME			YEAR						
ADDRESS			SENT	○	○	○	○	○	○
			RCVD	○	○	○	○	○	○

T

NAME		YEAR					
ADDRESS		SENT	○	○	○	○	○
		RCVD	○	○	○	○	○
NAME		YEAR					
ADDRESS		SENT	○	○	○	○	○
		RCVD	○	○	○	○	○
NAME		YEAR					
ADDRESS		SENT	○	○	○	○	○
		RCVD	○	○	○	○	○
NAME		YEAR					
ADDRESS		SENT	○	○	○	○	○
		RCVD	○	○	○	○	○
NAME		YEAR					
ADDRESS		SENT	○	○	○	○	○
		RCVD	○	○	○	○	○
NAME		YEAR					
ADDRESS		SENT	○	○	○	○	○
		RCVD	○	○	○	○	○
NAME		YEAR					
ADDRESS		SENT	○	○	○	○	○
		RCVD	○	○	○	○	○
NAME		YEAR					
ADDRESS		SENT	○	○	○	○	○
		RCVD	○	○	○	○	○
NAME		YEAR					
ADDRESS		SENT	○	○	○	○	○
		RCVD	○	○	○	○	○

NAME		YEAR						
ADDRESS		SENT	○	○	○	○	○	○
		RCVD	○	○	○	○	○	○
NAME		YEAR						
ADDRESS		SENT	○	○	○	○	○	○
		RCVD	○	○	○	○	○	○
NAME		YEAR						
ADDRESS		SENT	○	○	○	○	○	○
		RCVD	○	○	○	○	○	○
NAME		YEAR						
ADDRESS		SENT	○	○	○	○	○	○
		RCVD	○	○	○	○	○	○
NAME		YEAR						
ADDRESS		SENT	○	○	○	○	○	○
		RCVD	○	○	○	○	○	○
NAME		YEAR						
ADDRESS		SENT	○	○	○	○	○	○
		RCVD	○	○	○	○	○	○
NAME		YEAR						
ADDRESS		SENT	○	○	○	○	○	○
		RCVD	○	○	○	○	○	○
NAME		YEAR						
ADDRESS		SENT	○	○	○	○	○	○
		RCVD	○	○	○	○	○	○
NAME		YEAR						
ADDRESS		SENT	○	○	○	○	○	○
		RCVD	○	○	○	○	○	○

U

NAME		YEAR						
ADDRESS		SENT	○	○	○	○	○	○
		RCVD	○	○	○	○	○	○
NAME		YEAR						
ADDRESS		SENT	○	○	○	○	○	○
		RCVD	○	○	○	○	○	○
NAME		YEAR						
ADDRESS		SENT	○	○	○	○	○	○
		RCVD	○	○	○	○	○	○
NAME		YEAR						
ADDRESS		SENT	○	○	○	○	○	○
		RCVD	○	○	○	○	○	○
NAME		YEAR						
ADDRESS		SENT	○	○	○	○	○	○
		RCVD	○	○	○	○	○	○
NAME		YEAR						
ADDRESS		SENT	○	○	○	○	○	○
		RCVD	○	○	○	○	○	○
NAME		YEAR						
ADDRESS		SENT	○	○	○	○	○	○
		RCVD	○	○	○	○	○	○
NAME		YEAR						
ADDRESS		SENT	○	○	○	○	○	○
		RCVD	○	○	○	○	○	○
NAME		YEAR						
ADDRESS		SENT	○	○	○	○	○	○
		RCVD	○	○	○	○	○	○

NAME		YEAR						
ADDRESS		SENT	○	○	○	○	○	○
		RCVD	○	○	○	○	○	○
NAME		YEAR						
ADDRESS		SENT	○	○	○	○	○	○
		RCVD	○	○	○	○	○	○
NAME		YEAR						
ADDRESS		SENT	○	○	○	○	○	○
		RCVD	○	○	○	○	○	○
NAME		YEAR						
ADDRESS		SENT	○	○	○	○	○	○
		RCVD	○	○	○	○	○	○
NAME		YEAR						
ADDRESS		SENT	○	○	○	○	○	○
		RCVD	○	○	○	○	○	○
NAME		YEAR						
ADDRESS		SENT	○	○	○	○	○	○
		RCVD	○	○	○	○	○	○
NAME		YEAR						
ADDRESS		SENT	○	○	○	○	○	○
		RCVD	○	○	○	○	○	○
NAME		YEAR						
ADDRESS		SENT	○	○	○	○	○	○
		RCVD	○	○	○	○	○	○
NAME		YEAR						
ADDRESS		SENT	○	○	○	○	○	○
		RCVD	○	○	○	○	○	○

U

NAME		YEAR						
ADDRESS		SENT	○	○	○	○	○	○
		RCVD	○	○	○	○	○	○
NAME		YEAR						
ADDRESS		SENT	○	○	○	○	○	○
		RCVD	○	○	○	○	○	○
NAME		YEAR						
ADDRESS		SENT	○	○	○	○	○	○
		RCVD	○	○	○	○	○	○
NAME		YEAR						
ADDRESS		SENT	○	○	○	○	○	○
		RCVD	○	○	○	○	○	○
NAME		YEAR						
ADDRESS		SENT	○	○	○	○	○	○
		RCVD	○	○	○	○	○	○
NAME		YEAR						
ADDRESS		SENT	○	○	○	○	○	○
		RCVD	○	○	○	○	○	○
NAME		YEAR						
ADDRESS		SENT	○	○	○	○	○	○
		RCVD	○	○	○	○	○	○
NAME		YEAR						
ADDRESS		SENT	○	○	○	○	○	○
		RCVD	○	○	○	○	○	○
NAME		YEAR						
ADDRESS		SENT	○	○	○	○	○	○
		RCVD	○	○	○	○	○	○

U

NAME	DEAN & SYLVIA VILANDER	YEAR	2018	2019	20	21	22	23
ADDRESS	906 SE RASMUSSEN BLVD	SENT	✓	✓	✓	✓	✓	✓
	BATTLEGROUND W 98604	RCVD	✓	✓	✓	✓	✓	✓
NAME		YEAR						
ADDRESS		SENT						
		RCVD						
NAME		YEAR						
ADDRESS		SENT						
		RCVD						
NAME		YEAR						
ADDRESS		SENT						
		RCVD						
NAME		YEAR						
ADDRESS		SENT						
		RCVD						
NAME		YEAR						
ADDRESS		SENT						
		RCVD						
NAME		YEAR						
ADDRESS		SENT						
		RCVD						
NAME		YEAR						
ADDRESS		SENT						
		RCVD						
NAME		YEAR						
ADDRESS		SENT						
		RCVD						

NAME		YEAR					
ADDRESS		SENT	○	○	○	○	○	○
		RCVD	○	○	○	○	○	○
NAME		YEAR					
ADDRESS		SENT	○	○	○	○	○	○
		RCVD	○	○	○	○	○	○
NAME		YEAR					
ADDRESS		SENT	○	○	○	○	○	○
		RCVD	○	○	○	○	○	○
NAME		YEAR					
ADDRESS		SENT	○	○	○	○	○	○
		RCVD	○	○	○	○	○	○
NAME		YEAR					
ADDRESS		SENT	○	○	○	○	○	○
		RCVD	○	○	○	○	○	○
NAME		YEAR					
ADDRESS		SENT	○	○	○	○	○	○
		RCVD	○	○	○	○	○	○
NAME		YEAR					
ADDRESS		SENT	○	○	○	○	○	○
		RCVD	○	○	○	○	○	○
NAME		YEAR					
ADDRESS		SENT	○	○	○	○	○	○
		RCVD	○	○	○	○	○	○
NAME		YEAR					
ADDRESS		SENT	○	○	○	○	○	○
		RCVD	○	○	○	○	○	○

V

NAME		YEAR						
ADDRESS		SENT	○	○	○	○	○	○
		RCVD	○	○	○	○	○	○
NAME		YEAR						
ADDRESS		SENT	○	○	○	○	○	○
		RCVD	○	○	○	○	○	○
NAME		YEAR						
ADDRESS		SENT	○	○	○	○	○	○
		RCVD	○	○	○	○	○	○
NAME		YEAR						
ADDRESS		SENT	○	○	○	○	○	○
		RCVD	○	○	○	○	○	○
NAME		YEAR						
ADDRESS		SENT	○	○	○	○	○	○
		RCVD	○	○	○	○	○	○
NAME		YEAR						
ADDRESS		SENT	○	○	○	○	○	○
		RCVD	○	○	○	○	○	○
NAME		YEAR						
ADDRESS		SENT	○	○	○	○	○	○
		RCVD	○	○	○	○	○	○
NAME		YEAR						
ADDRESS		SENT	○	○	○	○	○	○
		RCVD	○	○	○	○	○	○
NAME		YEAR						
ADDRESS		SENT	○	○	○	○	○	○
		RCVD	○	○	○	○	○	○

V

NAME		YEAR						
ADDRESS		SENT	○	○	○	○	○	○
		RCVD	○	○	○	○	○	○
NAME		YEAR						
ADDRESS		SENT	○	○	○	○	○	○
		RCVD	○	○	○	○	○	○
NAME		YEAR						
ADDRESS		SENT	○	○	○	○	○	○
		RCVD	○	○	○	○	○	○
NAME		YEAR						
ADDRESS		SENT	○	○	○	○	○	○
		RCVD	○	○	○	○	○	○
NAME		YEAR						
ADDRESS		SENT	○	○	○	○	○	○
		RCVD	○	○	○	○	○	○
NAME		YEAR						
ADDRESS		SENT	○	○	○	○	○	○
		RCVD	○	○	○	○	○	○
NAME		YEAR						
ADDRESS		SENT	○	○	○	○	○	○
		RCVD	○	○	○	○	○	○
NAME		YEAR						
ADDRESS		SENT	○	○	○	○	○	○
		RCVD	○	○	○	○	○	○
NAME		YEAR						
ADDRESS		SENT	○	○	○	○	○	○
		RCVD	○	○	○	○	○	○

NAME	YEAR						
ADDRESS	SENT	○	○	○	○	○	○
	RCVD	○	○	○	○	○	○
NAME	YEAR						
ADDRESS	SENT	○	○	○	○	○	○
	RCVD	○	○	○	○	○	○
NAME	YEAR						
ADDRESS	SENT	○	○	○	○	○	○
	RCVD	○	○	○	○	○	○
NAME	YEAR						
ADDRESS	SENT	○	○	○	○	○	○
	RCVD	○	○	○	○	○	○
NAME	YEAR						
ADDRESS	SENT	○	○	○	○	○	○
	RCVD	○	○	○	○	○	○
NAME	YEAR						
ADDRESS	SENT	○	○	○	○	○	○
	RCVD	○	○	○	○	○	○
NAME	YEAR						
ADDRESS	SENT	○	○	○	○	○	○
	RCVD	○	○	○	○	○	○
NAME	YEAR						
ADDRESS	SENT	○	○	○	○	○	○
	RCVD	○	○	○	○	○	○
NAME	YEAR						
ADDRESS	SENT	○	○	○	○	○	○
	RCVD	○	○	○	○	○	○

W

NAME		YEAR						
ADDRESS		SENT	○	○	○	○	○	○
		RCVD	○	○	○	○	○	○
NAME		YEAR						
ADDRESS		SENT	○	○	○	○	○	○
		RCVD	○	○	○	○	○	○
NAME		YEAR						
ADDRESS		SENT	○	○	○	○	○	○
		RCVD	○	○	○	○	○	○
NAME		YEAR						
ADDRESS		SENT	○	○	○	○	○	○
		RCVD	○	○	○	○	○	○
NAME		YEAR						
ADDRESS		SENT	○	○	○	○	○	○
		RCVD	○	○	○	○	○	○
NAME		YEAR						
ADDRESS		SENT	○	○	○	○	○	○
		RCVD	○	○	○	○	○	○
NAME		YEAR						
ADDRESS		SENT	○	○	○	○	○	○
		RCVD	○	○	○	○	○	○
NAME		YEAR						
ADDRESS		SENT	○	○	○	○	○	○
		RCVD	○	○	○	○	○	○
NAME		YEAR						
ADDRESS		SENT	○	○	○	○	○	○
		RCVD	○	○	○	○	○	○

NAME		YEAR						
ADDRESS		SENT	○	○	○	○	○	○
		RCVD	○	○	○	○	○	○
NAME		YEAR						
ADDRESS		SENT	○	○	○	○	○	○
		RCVD	○	○	○	○	○	○
NAME		YEAR						
ADDRESS		SENT	○	○	○	○	○	○
		RCVD	○	○	○	○	○	○
NAME		YEAR						
ADDRESS		SENT	○	○	○	○	○	○
		RCVD	○	○	○	○	○	○
NAME		YEAR						
ADDRESS		SENT	○	○	○	○	○	○
		RCVD	○	○	○	○	○	○
NAME		YEAR						
ADDRESS		SENT	○	○	○	○	○	○
		RCVD	○	○	○	○	○	○
NAME		YEAR						
ADDRESS		SENT	○	○	○	○	○	○
		RCVD	○	○	○	○	○	○
NAME		YEAR						
ADDRESS		SENT	○	○	○	○	○	○
		RCVD	○	○	○	○	○	○
NAME		YEAR						
ADDRESS		SENT	○	○	○	○	○	○
		RCVD	○	○	○	○	○	○

X Y Z

NAME		YEAR					
ADDRESS		SENT	○	○	○	○	○	○
		RCVD	○	○	○	○	○	○
NAME		YEAR					
ADDRESS		SENT	○	○	○	○	○	○
		RCVD	○	○	○	○	○	○
NAME		YEAR					
ADDRESS		SENT	○	○	○	○	○	○
		RCVD	○	○	○	○	○	○
NAME		YEAR					
ADDRESS		SENT	○	○	○	○	○	○
		RCVD	○	○	○	○	○	○
NAME		YEAR					
ADDRESS		SENT	○	○	○	○	○	○
		RCVD	○	○	○	○	○	○
NAME		YEAR					
ADDRESS		SENT	○	○	○	○	○	○
		RCVD	○	○	○	○	○	○
NAME		YEAR					
ADDRESS		SENT	○	○	○	○	○	○
		RCVD	○	○	○	○	○	○
NAME		YEAR					
ADDRESS		SENT	○	○	○	○	○	○
		RCVD	○	○	○	○	○	○
NAME		YEAR					
ADDRESS		SENT	○	○	○	○	○	○
		RCVD	○	○	○	○	○	○

XYZ

NAME		YEAR						
ADDRESS		SENT	○	○	○	○	○	○
		RCVD	○	○	○	○	○	○
NAME		YEAR						
ADDRESS		SENT	○	○	○	○	○	○
		RCVD	○	○	○	○	○	○
NAME		YEAR						
ADDRESS		SENT	○	○	○	○	○	○
		RCVD	○	○	○	○	○	○
NAME		YEAR						
ADDRESS		SENT	○	○	○	○	○	○
		RCVD	○	○	○	○	○	○
NAME		YEAR						
ADDRESS		SENT	○	○	○	○	○	○
		RCVD	○	○	○	○	○	○
NAME		YEAR						
ADDRESS		SENT	○	○	○	○	○	○
		RCVD	○	○	○	○	○	○
NAME		YEAR						
ADDRESS		SENT	○	○	○	○	○	○
		RCVD	○	○	○	○	○	○
NAME		YEAR						
ADDRESS		SENT	○	○	○	○	○	○
		RCVD	○	○	○	○	○	○
NAME		YEAR						
ADDRESS		SENT	○	○	○	○	○	○
		RCVD	○	○	○	○	○	○

XY
Z

NAME		YEAR						
ADDRESS		SENT	○	○	○	○	○	○
		RCVD	○	○	○	○	○	○
NAME		YEAR						
ADDRESS		SENT	○	○	○	○	○	○
		RCVD	○	○	○	○	○	○
NAME		YEAR						
ADDRESS		SENT	○	○	○	○	○	○
		RCVD	○	○	○	○	○	○
NAME		YEAR						
ADDRESS		SENT	○	○	○	○	○	○
		RCVD	○	○	○	○	○	○
NAME		YEAR						
ADDRESS		SENT	○	○	○	○	○	○
		RCVD	○	○	○	○	○	○
NAME		YEAR						
ADDRESS		SENT	○	○	○	○	○	○
		RCVD	○	○	○	○	○	○
NAME		YEAR						
ADDRESS		SENT	○	○	○	○	○	○
		RCVD	○	○	○	○	○	○
NAME		YEAR						
ADDRESS		SENT	○	○	○	○	○	○
		RCVD	○	○	○	○	○	○
NAME		YEAR						
ADDRESS		SENT	○	○	○	○	○	○
		RCVD	○	○	○	○	○	○

XYZ

Discover more journals for your life!

www.JournalsOnAmazon.com

Made in the USA
San Bernardino, CA
27 December 2018